COLOR
ME A RHYME

Nature Poems for Young People by Jane Yolen

Photographs by
Jason Stemple

Wordsong/Boyds Mills Press

Text copyright © 2000 by Jane Yolen
Photographs copyright © 2000 by Jason Stemple

Published by Wordsong
Boyds Mills Press, Inc.
A Highlights Company
815 Church Street
Honesdale, Pennsylvania 18431
Prinied in China

U.S. Cataloging-in-Publication Data
  (Library of Congress Standards)
Yolen, Jane.
    Color me a rhyme : nature poems for young people / by Jane Yolen ;
photographs by Jason Stemple.—1st ed.
[32]p. : col. illus. ; cm.
Summary: Poems that celebrate the colors of nature.
ISBN: 1-56397-892-X hc   1-59078-172-4 pb
1. Nature—Poetry. 2. American poetry—20th century. I. Stemple, Jason.
II. Title.
811.54—21 2000 AC CIP
99-68893

First edition, 2000   First Boyds Mills Press paperback edition, 2003
Book designed by Jason Thorne
The text of this book is set in 18-point Palatino.

Visit our Web site at www.boydsmillspress.com

10 9 8 7 6 hc   10 9 8 7 6 5 4 3 2 pb

For Joanne Lee,
who always looks for rainbows — J.Y.

And who helps me see all the colors — J.S.

Contents

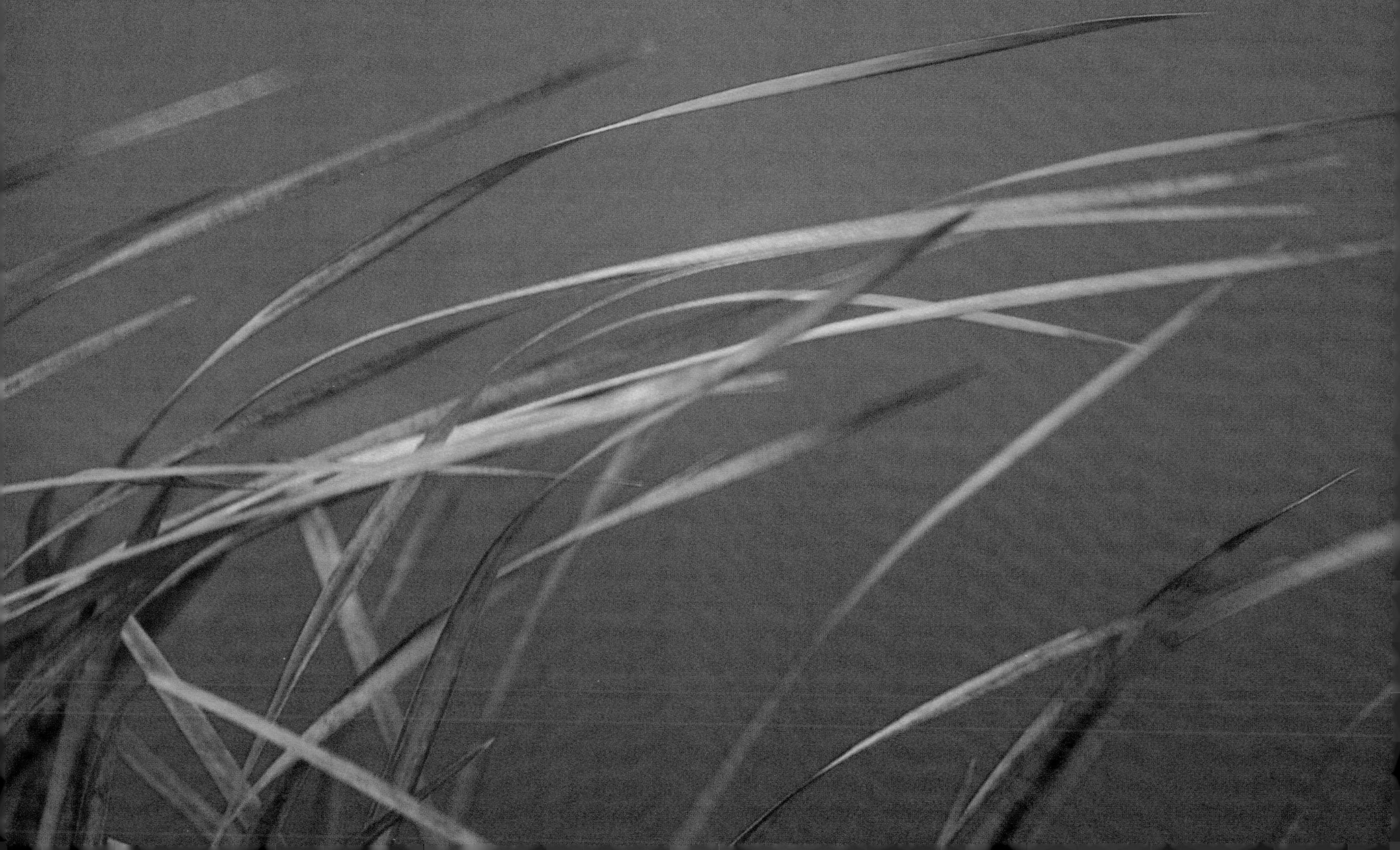

A Note from the Author

When Jason Stemple and I discussed this book, I said, "Find me colors in nature!" He laughed. He knew as I did that there are colors everywhere. The problem, of course, was not finding the colors, but isolating them. He had to take pictures that emphasized one color over all the others.

So for two years he shot photographs—in the mountains of Colorado, in the hills of Massachusetts, in the desert of the Southwest. He chased rainbows—literally. While driving with friends, he sometimes coaxed them to pull over, jumping out of the car to shoot a rainbow, a patch of red berries, an old, graying piece of wood.

And then over the Internet he began to send me the photos he liked best. I got to choose the ones I liked and to write poems about the images I observed and imagined.

You can write poems from his photos, too. And as an added incentive, I have included extra "color" words to help you.

—Jane Yolen

Green

Whichever angel had the task
of naming greens, squatting
on the hard new ground,
robe guttering at his perfect feet,
did not do his work well.
He gave us *chartreuse, olive, leek,*
emerald, ivy, beryl.
But they are not nearly enough
when the world is so much green.
Ferns, trees, grass, stems,
petals, limbs, leaves,
the soft mallow inside

each piece of greenware
deserve separate names.
Perhaps the world needed
a poet, not an angel,
because poets know
all the secret words,
some of which they make up,
all of which are
green.

"Poems are green."
— Maddison Jane Piatt

ivy

verdure

pleasure

grass

leek

"Where the gray trout lies asleep . . ."

— James Hogg

Gray

Gray trout in the water,
Gray clouds in the skies
Are graceful memories
And gradual lies.

But nothing is grayer
Than a dead old tree,
Dim reminder of what green
Used to be.

"I never saw a purple cow . . ."
— Gelett Burgess

Purple

I have no rhyme for purple.
None.
But each purple flower in the forest
is a poem.

amethyst

lavender

orchid

plum

violet

wine

apricot pumpkin

carrot

copper

Orange

I want to take a bite
out of that sunset sky,
letting the orange juices
run down my chin,
spitting out the pulp
onto the rocks below.

White

A star fell from the sky one night
And landed in the forest, white
Against the green of leaf and vine.

The star, though fallen, still was bright;
It cast its reel of brilliant light
The dark woods to entwine.

Moral:
If you should fall from such a height,
Do not despair about your plight,
Just rise—
    and shine.

pearl

chalk

alabaster

snow

bone

light red

rose

blush

flush

salmon

Pink: A Haiku

A surge of sunlight
Shocks through stem and thistle hairs.
A punk pink hairdo.

ebony

sable

jet

sloe

ink coal

20

"Black am I and much admired . . ."
— Mother Goose

Black

What is blacker than an
Alligator's skin?
Some say that the dark
Goes all the way in.
But I have watched gator
With her smaller kin.
Those knobs as black
As hardened sin
Are one of nature's deep surprises,
Which well disguises
What lies with
In.

"As all looks yellow to the jaundic'd eye."
— Alexander Pope

Yellow: A Haiku

One yellow leaf, yes!
But on the tree, in the woods,
One fades into all.

Two Red Haiku

Red butterfly clings
to the sandy-colored wall.
My heart's heart on wings.

brick

crimson

henna rouge

"Any color so long as it's red . . ."
— Eugene Field

vermilion

scarlet

ruby

cherry

cerise

Still life out of doors:
Berries splatter blood on leaves.
What does death matter?

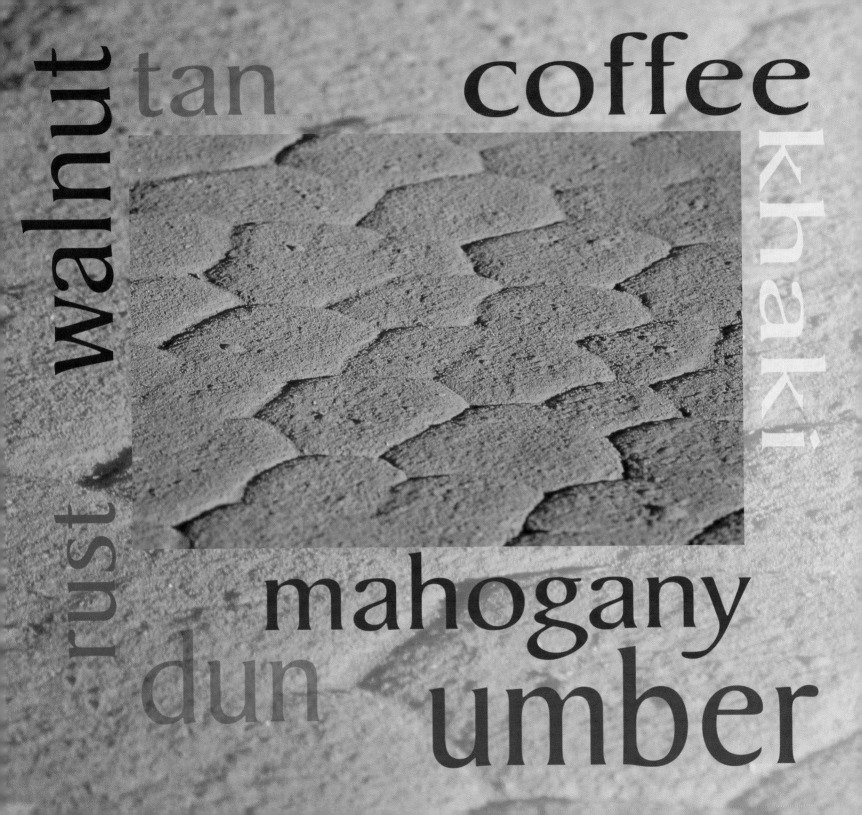

*"And thou art long,
and lank, and brown . . ."*
— Samuel Coleridge

Brown

In this brown desert
only earth matters.
There are no soft hills,
no soft folding land,
only the hard silence.
Here jigsaw shapes,
turned and baked
to a crust
by wind and sun,
expose a great puzzle:

Are we that earth,
across which runs
an occasional shadow,
or are we the shadow?

sapphire

cerulean

turquoise

azure

sky

B l u e

Clear sky slate.
Bird calligraphy.
A poem in flight.

Crayons: A Rainbow Poem

This box contains the wash of blue sky,
spikes of green spring,
a circle of yellow sun,
triangle flames of orange and red.

It has the lime caterpillar
inching on a brown branch,
the shadow black in the center
of a grove of trees.

It holds my pink
and your chocolate
and her burnt sienna
and his ivory skin.

In it are all the colors of the world.

All
the
colors
of
the
world.